Collins COBUILD

Dictionary Workbook

GW00727953

THE UNIVERSITY
OF BIRMINGHAM

COLLINS
COBUILD

HarperCollins*Publishers*

second edition 2001

© **HarperCollins Publishers 1995, 2001**

HarperCollins Publishers
Westerhill Road, Bishopbriggs, Glasgow G64 2QT

ISBN 0-00-711788-4

Collins®, COBUILD® and Bank of English® are registered
trademarks of HarperCollins Publishers Limited

www.cobuild.collins.co.uk

Corpus Acknowledgements

We would like to acknowledge the assistance of the many hundreds of individuals and
companies who have kindly given permission for copyright material to be used in
The Bank of English. The written sources include many national and regional
newspapers in Britain and overseas; magazine and periodical publishers; and book
publishers in Britain, the United States and Australia. Extensive spoken data has been
provided by radio and television broadcasting companies; research workers at many
universities and other institutions; and numerous individual contributors.
We are grateful to them all.

Author Acknowledgement

We would like to thank the author of the first edition of the COBUILD English
Dictionary Workbook, Malcolm Goodale, for his work in creating the original text,
on which we have based this edition.

Note

Entered words that we have reason to believe constitute trademarks have been
designated as such. However, neither the presence nor the absence of such designation
should be regarded as affecting the legal status of any trademark.

Typeset by Carol MacLeod
Printed in Great Britain by Montgomery Litho Group

Contents

SECTIONS

SECTION 1: FINDING WORDS AND PHRASES

SECTION 2: USING THE EXPLANATIONS AND EXAMPLES

SECTION 3: USING THE GRAMMATICAL INFORMATION

SECTION 4: USING THE PHONETICS

SECTION 5: LOOKING AT MEANING

SECTION 6: LOOKING AT VERY COMMON WORDS

Introduction

The **Collins COBUILD Dictionary Workbook** is designed to be used with the **Collins COBUILD English Dictionary for Advanced Learners**. The text for this new third edition of the COBUILD dictionary has been thoroughly revised and updated, and includes comprehensive coverage of American English. The explanations are given in full sentences for maximum clarity, and all the examples have been taken from the Bank of English, to show English as it is really used. The **Collins COBUILD English Dictionary for Advanced Learners** is also available on CD-ROM, together with a thesaurus, 5-million word Wordbank, extensive audio pronunciations, and a comprehensive guide to English Grammar and Usage.

The aim of the **Collins COBUILD Dictionary Workbook** is to help develop students' dictionary skills by showing them how they can make best use of the information given in the dictionary to produce natural language. We are sure that by working through the exercises in the workbook the students will gain a greater understanding of the language, and so increase their confidence in writing and speaking real English.

All the material in this workbook may be photocopied within an institution, and can be used in the classroom or for self-study.

Cobuild*Direct* —> online access to the Bank of English

Now you can tap into the Bank of English, the unique language resource on which the highly successful range of COBUILD dictionaries, grammars and other ELT publications is based.

Cobuild*Direct* is an online Internet service for accessing language data based on the Bank of English corpus of modern, written and spoken text. The key facilities are:

* Use of COBUILD's search and analysis software to extract concordances, word frequency and distribution statistics, collocation profiles and other data from a subset of the Bank of English corpus.

* Online searching of the Collins COBUILD English Dictionary

* A simple point-and-click interface to select word frequency lists and search on word patterns, word class and frequency.

Find out more at **www.cobuild.collins.co.uk**

Alphabetical Ordering

The Alphabet

Finding words in a dictionary is not always easy. Even native speakers sometimes fail to find words that are there.

If your own language is written in Roman script, you will be used to looking up words in alphabetical order. If your own language is written in a different script, you may find it more difficult to look up words in the Roman alphabet.

Write out the letters of the alphabet as they are ordered in English in the table below. You can consult this table later if you need to.

1	2	3	4	5	6	7	8	9	10	11	12	13
A												

14	15	16	17	18	19	20	21	22	23	24	25	26

Alphabetical Disorder!

Put these words in the correct alphabetical order:

distinguished	1	_____
distinctive	2	_____
disintegrate	3	_____
disinterested	4	_____
district	5	_____
distribution	6	_____
distributor	7	_____
destruction	8	_____
destructive	9	_____
distortion	10	_____

Compounds

Compound words (such as *breakfast time* and *breakfast television*) are very common in English, and this dictionary has a lot of useful information about them. These word combinations have a main entry when they are thought of as 'compounds' by native speakers. This means that native speakers think of the word combination as if it were one word in meaning. Some of these compounds have become one word.

Compounds (continued)

1   Compounds and Alphabetical Ordering

Compounds follow the usual rules for alphabetical ordering. These words all begin
with **brea**. Put them in alphabetical order, then check in the dictionary:

breadboard	1 _____	breaking point	6 _____
breakfast time	2 _____	breakfast	7 _____
bread	3 _____	breadth	8 _____
breakdown	4 _____	bread and butter	9 _____
break-in	5 _____	breakfast television	10 _____

2   How to Write Compounds

How are two-word expressions written? There are three possibilities:

Two words	tail end
With a hyphen	tail-light
One word	tailgate

Sometimes there is more than one possibility for a compound. In this case the
dictionary gives you the most common use first and then tells you about the
alternative spelling. Look at this entry for **breakfast time**:

> **breakfast time** also breakfast-time. Breakfast   N-UNCOUNT:
> time is the period of the morning when most people   oft prep N
> have their breakfast. ❑ *By breakfast-time he was already*
> *at his desk.*

This is a very difficult area of English, and the language is constantly changing. What
often happens is that a compound starts as two words, is then hyphenated, and finally
ends up as one word.

Imagine that the word **night** is attached to each of the following words. How would
you write it? Then check your answers in the dictionary.

1 _____ club		5 _____ owl
2 _____ gown		6 _____ time
3 _____ life		7 _____ watchman
4 _____ mare		

Some compounds are also written differently in American English. Look in your
dictionary for the alternative American spellings for the following:

8 apple sauce _____	10 knick-knacks _____
9 check-up _____	11 mark-up _____

Choose any two pages of the dictionary and see how many compounds you can find.

Spelling

Looking up a word in the dictionary is easy if you are quite certain how it is spelled. But one important use of the dictionary is to check spellings that you are not certain about.

1   A or E?

Have you ever confused these two words?   *affect/effect*

Complete the beginning of the words in these sentences, using either the word **affect** or the word **effect**. When you've finished, check your answers in the dictionary.

1   Susan was greatly ___ffected by his death.
2   His death had a terrible ___ffect on her.
3   When does the new law come into ___ffect?
4   Arthritis is a crippling disease which ___ffects people all over the world.
5   It's certainly going to ___ffect our budget for next year.

2   Confused Spellings

Small spelling differences in words which are pronounced the same or almost the same are difficult even for native speakers. Sometimes the words have completely different meanings, but sometimes their meanings are related in some way. Often the difference is also a difference of grammar. For example, the meanings of **practise** and **practice** are related, but **practise** is a verb, and **practice** is a noun. However, the words **stationary** and **stationery** are not related at all in meaning.

The next exercise contains pairs of easily confusable words. Each word has one or more letters missing. Complete the words with the missing letters. Under each pair of words are two examples with one of the two words missing. Choose the correct word from each pair for each example. Then check your answers in the dictionary.

1   princip____/princip____
     a   His _____ interest in life was to be rich.
     b   ... the _____ of acceleration.

2   practi___e/practi___e
     a   Many doctors _____ from their own houses.
     b   ... a doctor with a private _____.

3   station___ry/station___ry
     a   Use the handbrake when your vehicle is _____.
     b   He had a shop which sold _____.

4   comp___ment/comp___ment
     a   He was a perfect contrast and _____ to Sally.
     b   Thanks for the _____.

Rules for spelling in English are complicated. However, when you cannot find a word and you think that is because you cannot spell it properly, you can try:

1   Asking yourself if you are pronouncing the word properly.
2   Writing down possible spellings, crossing out unlikely ones and looking up the rest.

Phrases 1

In English there are a lot of expressions which consist of two or more words. Many of these are phrasal verbs, which are dealt with later on. Many others are expressions or fixed phrases. The dictionary contains explanations of many of these expressions but it is sometimes difficult to know where to find them.

How to Find Phrases

Here is part of the dictionary entry for **mouth**:

> **9** If you **keep** your **mouth shut** about something, you do not talk about it, especially because it is a secret. □ *You wouldn't be here now if she'd kept her mouth shut.* PHRASE: V and N inflect = keep quiet
>
> **10** → **live hand to mouth**: see **hand**. → **heart in your mouth**: see **heart**. → **from the horse's mouth**: see **horse**. → **to put your money where your mouth is**: see **money**. → **shut your mouth**: see **shut**. → **born with a silver spoon in your mouth**: see **spoon**. → **word of mouth**: see **word**. → **put words into** someone's **mouth**: see **word**.

As you can see from the paragraph numbers (9 and 10), phrases come at the end of the entry for **mouth**. You will also see that in paragraph 9, the phrase **keep** your **mouth shut** is explained, but in paragraph 10 the phrases are not explained. You are given an instruction to 'see ...'. This means that if you want to know more about the phrase **born with a silver spoon in** your **mouth**, you have to look up the word **spoon**.

Phrases are usually explained at the least common word or at the noun, and this is why **born with a silver spoon in** your **mouth** is explained at **spoon** and not at **mouth**.

Which entry would you look up to find the explanations for the following phrases?

1   a blessing in disguise   _____

2   the good old days   _____

3   to hate someone's guts   _____

4   to give the game away   _____

5   only a matter of time   _____

Phrases 2

Eye

Look at the entry for **eye**. This is a word which is used in a large number of phrases; some are explained at **eye** and others are cross-referenced to other words in the dictionary.

The examples in the following table all contain phrases using the word **eye**. First, look at the entry for **eye** to find out where each phrase is explained. Look up each phrase, and then fill in the table, saying where the phrase is explained and giving its paragraph number. Then write the phrase itself. The first one is done for you.

Example	Word at which phrase is explained	Paragraph number	Phrase
1 Just this once, we'll turn a blind eye to what you've done.	**blind**	**11**	**turn a blind eye**
2 Keep an eye on him for me while I'm away, would you?			
3 The flowers in the window caught my eye.			
4 I wanted to explain what had happened, but I couldn't catch Mr Craig's eye.			
5 Stop trying to pull the wool over my eyes! What were you two fighting about just now?			
6 In the corner a little girl was crying her eyes out.			
7 I lost my temper and gave him a black eye.			
8 The planet Mars will be visible to the naked eye all week.			

Phrases 3

View

Look at the dictionary for the word **view**. Complete the following sentences, using one of the following phrases:

in my view   in view of   with a view to   in view   on view

1   _____ the fact that she was first, she should get the prize.

2   The journalist wrote the story _____ embarrassing the government.

3   We are, _____ , still no further forward.

4   In the Van Gogh Museum in Amsterdam, 130 of his paintings are _____.

5   They worked out this whole complicated plot with one aim _____ — to gain control of the company.

6   _____ the team should have acted sooner.

Phrasal Verbs

It is important to realize that phrasal verbs listed in the dictionary appear together at the end of the entry of the verb from which they are formed. Phrasal verbs come before any other words which occur alphabetically after the verb. This is to make it easier for you to find these very common expressions.

1   Phrasal Verbs with Break

Look up the phrasal verbs that start with the verb **break**.

1   How many different meanings of **break away** are given?   _____

2   Which paragraph of **break down** has a machine as the subject of the verb?   _____

3   Which paragraphs of **break down** mention a person as the subject of the verb?   _____

4   Which paragraph of **break in** has a cross-reference?   _____

5   Which phrasal verb in the dictionary comes before the phrasal verb **break up**?   _____

6   Which entry in the dictionary comes after the phrasal verb **break up**?   _____

7   Make a list of all the phrasal verbs that start with the verb **break**:

_____   _____

_____   _____

_____   _____

_____   _____

2   Phrasal Verbs with Get

Match the following sentences to each of the meanings of **get out**. There is one example for each meaning.

Example   **Paragraph Number**

1   We don't get out much together, what with the children being so young.   _____

2   If this gets out, we'll lose the contract.   _____

3   They can't get out, the army has them surrounded.   _____

4   I can't get out of it, we have an agreement.   _____

10

SECTION 2: USING THE EXPLANATIONS AND EXAMPLES

Someone and Something

In this dictionary, the explanation of a word and the examples that follow it do not only give you information about the meaning of the word; they also often give you information about how the word is typically used.

The exercises in this section show you how to use this information in order to get the best out of your dictionary.

People or Things

Some words are used mainly of people, while others are used mainly of objects or ideas. The explanations and examples tell you whether a word is normally found in one kind of context only.

Look up the word **incapable** and decide which of these sentences it is likely to be used in.

a   The car was _____ of being mended.

b   She was _____ of stealing.

Each explanation in the dictionary refers to 'someone' who is incapable, and all the examples describe people as incapable. This tells you that we normally use the word to describe people, not machines, which means that (b) is the correct answer.

Now do the same thing with each of the following words (be careful as one of the words can be used with both people and things!):

1   **unworkable**

a   She turned down all of his suggestions as _____ without giving them a try.

b   He is _____ in this company.

2   **rubbish**

a   He thought the film was absolute _____.

b   I love playing football but I'm _____ at it.

3   **insensitive**

a   This software is _____ to our needs.

b   I feel my husband is very _____ about my problem.

4   **cancerous**

a   The energy of the radiation will kill the _____ cells.

b   ...a hospital which specializes in the treatment of _____ patients.

Word Order

Some words or expressions are used in one position in a sentence more frequently than in any other position. It is not necessarily wrong to use them in another position but it may sound slightly strange or unnatural.

Word Order (continued)

1 The Position of Adverbs

Look up the word **increasingly** in the dictionary and then decide which position in the sentence it would most naturally fill. Choose from those places marked with an asterisk:

I * am * getting * unhappy * about the way things are developing.

The examples in the entry talk of things being increasingly difficult, increasingly popular, and so on. This tells you that **increasingly** is typically used immediately before an adjective or verb. The answer is therefore:

...getting **increasingly** unhappy...

Now do the same thing with each of the following words:

1 **incomparably**   We * are * better off * than we were a year ago.

2 **particularly**   They don't go out much, * during the winter months *.

3 **incredibly**   The film * was * boring.

2 The Order of Adjectives

When there is more than one adjective before a noun, this is the order they go in:

He showed me two very *large white wooden* boxes.

Large is a graded adjective. A graded adjective can be used with an adverb or phrase indicating degree, such as *less, more, very,* etc. Many graded adjectives have comparative and superlative forms.

Large is noted in the Extra Column as: ADJ-GRADED

White is noted in the Extra Column as: COLOUR

Wooden is an ungraded adjective. Ungraded adjectives are very rarely used with an adverb or phrase indicating degree, e.g., *He has been <u>absent</u> for two weeks.*

Wooden is noted in the Extra Column as: ADJ

Now put these adjectives in the correct order in the following sentences.

1 **French, small**   Her family ran a _____ _____ restaurant in the theatrical district of the city.

2 **soft, yellow**   The small lamp on the table made a _____ _____ glow all around her.

3 **gilt, huge**   _____ _____ earrings dangled from her ears.

4 **white, woollen**   The baby was wrapped in a _____ _____ shawl.

5 **long, unbroken**   In the _____ _____ silence which followed she realized that he had fallen asleep.

6 **check, old, pink**   A potted plant stood on the _____ _____ _____ cloth.

Verbs

1   Verbs and their Subjects

Apart from the meaning, a great deal of other information is given in the explanation of the words. Look at the way verbs are explained in the dictionary.

> A   If the verb refers to something that most people might do, the explanation usually begins 'If you ...'. For example, 'If you **ask** someone something, you say something to them in the form of a question ...'.

> B   If the verb refers to something that few people do or that we think people should not be encouraged to do, the explanation usually begins 'If someone ...'. For example, 'If someone or something **bores** you, you find them dull and uninteresting'.

> C   If the subject of the verb is usually not a person but a thing, the explanation begins 'If something ...'. For example, 'If something **adheres** to something else, it sticks firmly to it.'

You will also find that the explanations of some verbs begin in other ways in the dictionary. Try to think why those particular words have been used.

Which of the three forms of words that have been explained above do you think are used in the dictionary in the following sentences? Look in the dictionary to check.

Examples	**A, B, or C?**	**Examples**	**A, B, or C?**
1 He *kicked* the window open.	___	4 He *nodded* his head.	___
2 She wanted to *borrow* my book.	___	5 The strange noise *alarmed* me.	___
3 They started to *swear* and shout.	___	6 Bombs *obliterated* the villages.	___

2   When or If?

Now look at another feature of the way verbs are explained in the dictionary:

> A   If the verb refers to something that someone regularly or typically does, the explanation usually begins 'When ...'. For example, 'When you **cough**, you force air out of your throat with a sudden, harsh noise ...'.

> B   If the verb refers to something that someone does only occasionally, or that not everyone does, the explanation usually begins 'If ...'. For example, 'If you **resign** from a job or position, you formally announce that you are leaving it.'

Which of the two forms of words that have been used above do you think are used in the dictionary in the following sentences? Look in the dictionary to check.

Examples	**A or B?**
1 Relax your muscles and *breathe* deeply.	_____
2 He *died* in 1987, aged seventy.	_____
3 Then she *broke down* in tears.	_____
4 One day a larger ship *anchored* offshore.	_____
5 The authorities had taken the decision to *deport* him.	_____

Collocations 1

Collocations are words that go together. It is not always enough to know the meaning of a word for you to be able to use it appropriately. You have to know the collocates of the word: the words that most frequently occur with it. The dictionary gives a lot of information on collocations. Look at the following paragraphs from **fast**.

> **6** If you hold **fast** to a principle or idea, or if you stand **fast**, you do not change your mind about it, even though people are trying to persuade you to. ❑ *We can only try to hold fast to the age-old values of honesty, decency and concern for others... He told supporters to stand fast over the next few vital days.*
>
> ADV-GRADED:
> ADV after v
> = firmly

This tells you that two verbs (**hold** and **stand**) are usually used with this meaning of **fast**.

> **10** Someone who is **fast asleep** is completely asleep. ❑ *When he went upstairs five minutes later, she was fast asleep.*
>
> PHRASE:
> v-link PHR,
> PHR after v

Here the collocation is a phrase and is therefore in bold: **fast asleep**.

1 Adjectives

Many adjectives in English are used with only a small selection of nouns. Using the information in the explanations and examples, say what sorts of words these adjectives are used with. The first one has been done for you.

1 scorching   **weather, temperatures, day** _____

2 daunting   _____

3 auburn   _____

4 purpose-built   _____

5 back-breaking   _____

2 Adverbs and Adjectives

Some adverbs and adjectives are very commonly used with only one other word. You will often find that they are used in this way simply to give emphasis to the word that follows. For example, if someone is **dead tired**, they are very tired indeed.

Sometimes these collocations are shown as phrases in the dictionary, and sometimes they are shown in the explanations.

Use the dictionary to help you fill in the missing words below.

1 I've been awake since dawn. Chris is still sound _____ in the other bed.

2 His other inventions have hardly been a roaring _____.

3 They were filthy _____. They had a huge house in the south of France.

4 Now I've got my own house I'm always flat _____.

Collocations 2

Common Verbs and Nouns

Many common verbs like **do**, **have**, **make**, **set**, and **take** form collocations with certain nouns. In these collocations, most of the meaning is carried by the nouns they are associated with.

<u>Underline</u> the verb + noun collocations in these examples.

1   He would never have thought of making a telephone call to the police to tell them where it was.
2   There may be other ways to persuade students to do homework without making it compulsory.
3   Sorry, we made a mistake. Your blood test got mixed up with someone else's.
4   Should the Royal Family set an example when it comes to marriage?
5   Tomorrow afternoon we'll return the library books and do some shopping!

Now complete the following quotations and newspaper headlines using the correct form of **do**, **make**, **give**, or **hold**.

6   I hate housework. You _____ the beds, you _____ the dishes. And six months later you have to start all over again. *Joan Rivers*
7   If I wasn't _____ mistakes, I wasn't _____ decisions. *Robert W. Johnson*
8   Brazil's new president _____ first speech.
9   Mia Farrow _____ star performance in court.
10 Somalia's factions _____ peace talks.

Style and Usage 1

1   Style and Register

A lot of words and expressions in English can be used in one kind of situation, but not in others. Many words are found in particular kinds of English, such as formal, informal, technical, literary, or old-fashioned language, or only in American or British English. The dictionary gives you this information, in addition to telling you about the meaning. No additional information is given for words which are suitable for use in most contexts. Look up the following words in the dictionary and find out what the dictionary says about the way that they are used.

Word	Style & Register		Word	Style & Register
1 aubergine	_____	6	anterior	_____
2 bookstore	_____	7	decaf	_____
3 frock	_____	8	amortize	_____
4 belated	_____	9	bespectacled	_____
5 larceny	_____	10	besmirch	_____

Style and Usage 1 (continued)

2 Informal or Formal?

Look at the words in *italics* in these pairs of examples and say which ones you think are
informal. When you've finished, look them up in the dictionary to check your answers.

Examples   **a or b?**

1 a When I was a *child* I lived in a country village.
   b All the *kids* in my class could read.   _____
2 a He's living with his mum and *dad*.
   b He would be a good *father* to my children.   _____
3 a She turned the *television* on and started watching the news.
   b After a day's work most people want to relax in front of the *telly*. _____
4 a Beer costs three *pounds* a bottle.
   b It cost him five hundred *quid*.   _____

Style and Usage 2

American or British?

Look at the following entry in the dictionary to see how the differences between British
English and American English are shown.

> **leading article** (leading articles)   ◆◇◇◇◇
> [1] A **leading article** in a newspaper is a piece of writ- N-COUNT
> ing which gives the editor's opinion on an important
> news item. [BRIT]
> ✔ in AM, use **editorial**
> [2] A **leading article** in a newspaper is the most im- N-COUNT
> portant story in it. [AM]
> ✔ in BRIT, use **lead**

Now look at the following examples and say whether the word in *italics* is British English
or American English. Then write the equivalent word in the space provided. Use the
dictionary to help you.

Examples   **British or American   Equivalent**

1 This requires having a *tap* in the kitchen.   _____   _____

2 He raised the *hood* of McKee's truck.   _____   _____

3 Lock your valuables in the *boot*.   _____   _____

4 Charles walked slowly down the *sidewalk*.   _____   _____

5 He put on black *trousers* and a white shirt.   _____   _____

6 He had almost half a tank of *gasoline*.   _____   _____

7 I took the *elevator* to the twenty-first floor. _____   _____

8 Len first heard it while he was in the *queue*.   _____   _____

9 Under her bed was a stale chocolate *biscuit*.   _____   _____

10 An awful odor rose from the *garbage can*.   _____   _____

16

SECTION 3: USING THE GRAMMATICAL INFORMATION

Parts of Speech

The COBUILD *dictionary* does not *just give* you *information about* the *meaning of words*, it *also gives* you *useful information about* their *grammar*. This *information is shown clearly* and *concisely in* the Extra Column.

1   What Part of Speech is it?

Look back at the words in *italics* in the two sentences above and find examples of these parts of speech:

1 Nouns   _____

2 Verbs   _____

3 Adjectives   _____

4 Adverbs   _____

5 Prepositions   _____

2   Nouns, Verbs, Adjectives, Adverbs and Prepositions

Look up these words in the dictionary: **down**, **round**, **good**. Each of these words belongs to more than one word class. Write the correct word in the sentences below and give the word class:

1 a   As I drove _____ the mountain, day was ending.   _____

   b   They managed to _____ two bottles of wine.   _____

   c   He put the tray _____ on the table at her side.   _____

2 a   He's very _____ at telling people what they want to hear. _____

   b   She is too smart for her own _____.   _____

3 a   Sue got a sympathetic _____ of applause.   _____

   b   She had small feet and hands and a flat _____ face.   _____

   c   They needed some way of getting _____ the country.   _____

   d   ...a murderer waiting for his victim to _____ the corner. _____

Verbs

1   Verb Patterns

Here is a list of some of the main verb patterns that you will see in the dictionary. In each case capital **V** stands for the verb in the entry.

V	**V prep/adv**	**V with quote**
V that	**V n**	**V pron-refl**
V to-inf	**V -ing**	**V n n**
V n *into* **-ing**	**V n to-inf**	**V n adj**

Verbs (continued)

Look at these sentences and give each one the correct pattern. The first one has been done for you.

1   Her boyfriend *gave* her a diamond ring.   **V n n**

2   I *can't bear* to think of time passing.   _____

3   Please *cancel* my appointments for the rest of the day.   _____

4   He *glanced* at his watch.   _____

5   'I *disapprove* of hunting, myself,' she *said*.   _____

6   *Enjoy* yourself more.   _____

7   The accused refuses to *admit* that it was wrong to use force.   _____

8   The jury *found* her guilty of second-degree murder.   _____

9   One evening he *asked* me to go and have a drink with him.   _____

10 Henry *charmed* people into parting with thousands of pounds.   _____

11 My lawyer called the bank to find out what *had occurred*.   _____

12 She *regretted* having revealed so much of her life to him.   _____

2   Verbs Followed by Prepositional Phrases

Some verbs have the pattern **V prep**, or a pattern with a specified preposition such as **V *in* n**. Complete the following sentences with the correct preposition from the list below. When you've finished, look up the verbs in the dictionary to check your answers.

on	about	to	in	for	from

1   They *were arguing* _____ politics as they played.

2   The house *had belonged* _____ her family for three generations.

3   The Prime Minister *concentrated* particularly _____ the provisions made for women in the social charter.

4   After leaving university, Therese *decided* _____ a career in publishing.

5   The cooking time *depends* _____ the size of the potato.

6   I used to sit and *worry* _____ my future.

7   Money can't buy happiness, but it helps you *look* _____ it in a lot more places.

8   Criminals may be *prevented* _____ leaving the country.

9   They *objected* _____ the cigarette smoke with which he filled the room.

10 They *rely* _____ firewood for cooking.

11 All countries are expected to *succeed* _____ bringing down inflation this year.

Nouns 1

1   Count, Uncount and Variable Nouns

Look on pages xxvii and xxix of the Introduction to the dictionary for explanations of
N-COUNT, **N-UNCOUNT** and **N-VAR**. Then look at each of the sets of sentences
below and say which class the noun in *italics* belongs to. Check your answers in the
dictionary.

1   No one had lived in the house for decades, but it was still full of *furniture*.
    The *furniture* is a mixture of new and old.
    Every single piece of *furniture* is original.   _____

2   If today's talks lead to negotiations, a *compromise* is the most likely outcome.
    He is a cautious man who favours *compromise*.
    Have you had to make *compromises*?   _____

3   Healthy *bones* are among the benefits that can result from a balanced diet.
    One of the functions of *bone* is to store calcium.
    The cricketer broke a *bone* in his left hand.   _____

4   Do you feel the need for an *aim* in life?
    One of the *aims* of the study was to measure the effects of radiation.
    What was his main *aim* when he was setting it up?   _____

2   Nouns with Different Behaviour Patterns

Some nouns sometimes have different patterns from the normal behaviour for that
word class. This behaviour is shown in the dictionary with 'also'. Look up the words
lack and **paperback** in the dictionary and fit the words into the following sentences.

1   Too little eye contact might be regarded as a sign of dishonesty or _____
    of interest.

    A _____ of medicine was the reason for the deaths, he said.

2   On the table sits a _____ of his new autobiography.

    The book first began to make his reputation after it was published in _____
    in 1996.

Nouns 2

1   Noun Patterns 1

Here is a list of some of the noun patterns that you will see in the dictionary. In each
case, capital **N** stands for the noun in the entry.

poss N	**N n**	**n N**
N *for* n	**N to-inf**	

19

Nouns 2 (continued)

Look at these sentences and give each one the correct pattern. In each sentence, the noun in the entry is in *italics*.

1 The government honoured a *promise* to hold elections in 1997. _____

2 She remembered her *childhood* as being one long, sunny idyll. _____

3 We marched on to the *hilltop* village of Monteriggioni. _____

4 There was plenty of *opportunity* for discussion after the meeting. _____

5 He saved up to start his own business — a clothing *factory*. _____

2 Noun Patterns 2

Look on page xxxvi of the Introduction to the dictionary for explanations of **supp** and **poss** and their patterns. Then look at these sentences and underline the words which are part of the pattern.

1 **N with supp**
  a It folds away for storage — an *aspect* which most parents will find appealing.
  b Repeat the movement two or three times in the same *direction*.

2 **supp N**
  a Should America be giving humanitarian *aid*?
  b It had to be a man who knew the theatre *crowd*.

3 **N with poss**
  a He had recovered from the flight and the shock of his *arrival*.
  b Detroit was an ideal spot for the *birth* of the mass-produced automobile.

Adjectives 1

1 Graded and Ungraded Adjectives

Adjectives which are sometimes modified by a grading word such as *fairly, more, so,* or *very* (graded adjectives) are labelled **ADJ-GRADED** in the dictionary. Adjectives which are rarely or never modified in that way (ungraded adjectives) are labelled **ADJ** (see page xxv of the Introduction to the dictionary). Often, an adjective can be a graded adjective and an ungraded adjective in different senses. Look up the adjectives in *italics* in the sentences below and say whether the adjective is graded or ungraded.

1 a Most of the staff were *outgoing*, energetic, and enthusiastic. _____

  b In the *outgoing* national assembly, the party held 25 seats. _____

2 a The championships were run by the *athletic* club. _____

  b Barry was a pleasant, *athletic* sort of guy from New York. _____

3 a He was a *cold-blooded* businessman like his father. _____

  b Some *cold-blooded* fish can swim in sub-zero temperatures. _____

Adjectives 1 (continued)

2   Positions of Adjectives

In the dictionary, adjectives which always or usually come before nouns are labelled
ADJ n, and adjectives which always or usually come after link verbs are labelled **v-link
ADJ**. Adjectives which do not have either of these labels are used in both positions.
Look up the adjectives in these sentences and show whether they are **ADJ n**, **v-link
ADJ**, or **both**.

1   When I was a child I was *happy*.   _____

2   What Beth has said is *absolute* nonsense.   _____

3   At the end of 1986, Mr Gates took over as *acting* director.   _____

4   If you follow these simple guidelines you'll feel *better*.   _____

5   Are you a *tidy* person?   _____

6   What do you mean I've got money? I'm as *broke* as you are.   _____

Adjectives 2

1   Adjective Patterns 1

Here is a list of some of the main adjective patterns that you will see in the dictionary.
After each sentence, put in the appropriate adjective pattern. Remember that **that**
clauses do not always begin with the word *that*. When you've finished, look up the
adjectives in the dictionary to check your answers.

| ADJ *to* n | ADJ to-inf | *it* v-link ADJ to-inf |
| ADJ *of* n | ADJ that | |

1   He was as *blind* to her feelings as she was to his.   _____

2   'We are *glad* you could come,' said Leonard.   _____

3   They all greeted me very cordially and were *eager* to talk
    about the project.   _____

4   It is *difficult* to write and express gratitude to a person you
    don't know.   _____

5   He would not have recognized her, of that he felt *certain*.   _____

You can use the pattern ***it* v-link ADJ that** to introduce a comment that you want to
make, e.g. *it is clear that..., it is said that....*

Try to think of other similar patterns.

Adjectives 2 (continued)

2 Adjective Patterns 2

Here are some sentences which have been split apart and jumbled up. Draw arrows between the right and left hand parts to indicate which parts belong together. If you need to, look up the adjective in the dictionary, find the appropriate sense and find out which patterns it has.

1	They are cautiously *optimistic*	a	to be insulted in the street.
2	He was thought to be *fit*	b	with her husband's sales methods.
3	It cannot have been *pleasant*	c	that the improvement will be maintained.
4	She became *familiar*	d	in fruit and vegetables.
5	We are particularly *fond*	e	on a guarantee of safety.
6	He made his departure *conditional*	f	of listening to music.
7	His diet is *deficient*	g	to play at the weekend.

Adverbs

1 Adverb Patterns

Here is a list of some of the main adverb patterns.

ADV with v   ADV with cl   ADV adj/adv   ADV -ed

Match these patterns with the examples below. The adverb is in *italics* in each example. Then look up the adverbs in the dictionary to check your answers.

1 Since 1990, *however*, all member governments have expressed their support.
It was a brilliant film. *However*, the movie did have its critics.   _____

2 The commission *quickly* concluded that there was a need for change.
The known facts are few and can be summarized *quickly*.   _____

3 You know *perfectly* well what I mean.
Can you imagine throwing away a *perfectly* good book?   _____

4 During the first week, the classes were *poorly* attended.   _____

2 Just

Here is a list of the most common adverbial patterns of **just**.

ADV before v   ADV adv/prep   ADV n   ADV *about/going* to-inf

Match these patterns with the examples below. When you've finished, look up the first five adverb uses of **just1** in the dictionary to check your answers.

1 Randall would just now be getting the Sunday paper.   _____
2 The Vietnam War was just about to end.   _____
3 That's just one example of the kind of experiments you can do.   _____
4 I've just bought a new house.   _____

Consonants and Vowels

The spelling of English words is not always a good guide to how they are pronounced. For this reason, the dictionary shows you how to pronounce each word using the symbols of the International Phonetic Alphabet (IPA). A key to these symbols is given on page xxxviii of the dictionary.

1 Consonants

There are 25 consonant symbols. Most of the consonant symbols are written the same as normal letters, e.g. bed is written in phonetics like this: /b<u>e</u>d/. There are only eight consonants which have special symbols. These are:

/ ʃ ʒ ŋ tʃ θ ð dʒ j /

Match these special symbols with the words below. The sounds you are looking for are <u>underlined</u> and in **bold**.

	Word	Symbol			Word	Symbol
1	mea**s**ure	_____		5	**sh**ip	_____
2	**j**oy	_____		6	**th**in	_____
3	**y**ellow	_____		7	**th**en	_____
4	**ch**eap	_____		8	si**ng**	_____

2 Vowels

The most difficult symbols are the vowel symbols and there are 22 of them! Here we have divided them into three sections: short vowels, long vowels, and combinations of vowel sounds.

a Short Vowels   / æ e ɪ ɒ ʊ ʌ ə i u /

Each sentence below has at least three examples of one of the sounds above. Use your dictionary to match the sounds with the sentences.

		Symbol	How many?
1	Fit children have a winning system.	_____	_____
2	They could put the wood in the shed.	_____	_____
3	My friend said he went to bed wet.	_____	_____
4	The bad man sat on a mat.	_____	_____
5	Blood! I've cut myself! I must get some help.	_____	_____
6	The teacher is in danger.	_____	_____
7	I spotted a lot of lost dogs.	_____	_____
8	...factual errors about the actual number of casualties.	_____	_____
9	We created very many jobs.	_____	_____

Consonants and Vowels (continued)

b   **_Long Vowels_**   / ɑː iː ɔː uː ɜː /

Each sentence below has at least three examples of one of the sounds above. Use your dictionary to match the sounds with the sentences.

		Symbol	**How many?**
1	We beat the team.	_____	_____
2	More than four balls were caught.	_____	_____
3	At last my heart started to calm down.	_____	_____
4	The first bird earned the third worm.	_____	_____
5	You choose if we use the shoe or the boot.	_____	_____

c   **_Vowel Combinations_**   / aɪ aɪə aʊ aʊə eɪ eə ɪə ɔɪ oʊ ʊə /

Each sentence below has at least two examples of one of the sounds above. Use your dictionary to match the sounds with the sentences.

		Symbol	**How many?**
1	I'm sure a cure will help the poor.	_____	_____
2	After the fire it's difficult to find a buyer.	_____	_____
3	It's too loud. Turn it down now or get out!	_____	_____
4	A tower is a sign of power.	_____	_____
5	There must be a place we can get a beer near here.	_____	_____
6	Take care what you wear if you have fair hair.	_____	_____
7	They say steak makes you put on weight.	_____	_____
8	Give me your coat. There's a note by the phone for you.	_____	_____
9	The lawyer poisoned the boy.	_____	_____
10	I don't mind if you try, but why not buy a guide?	_____	_____

American and British Pronunciation

1   American Pronunciation

When American pronunciation differs from the usual British pronunciation, a separate transcription is given of the part of the word that is pronounced differently in American English.

Study this list of words and their phonetic transcriptions. Say each word both ways and decide which pronunciation is which. Write BRIT by the British pronunciation and AM by the American pronunciation.

1	advertisement	/ædvəˈtaɪzmənt/	_____	/ædvɜːˈtɪsmənt/	_____
2	missile	/mɪsaɪl/	_____	/mɪsᵊl/	_____
3	thorough	/θɜːroʊ/	_____	/θʌrə/	_____
4	tomato	/təmɑːtoʊ/	_____	/təmeɪtou/	_____
5	duty	/duːti/	_____	/djuːti/	_____

2   Alternative British Pronunciation

British speakers also pronounce words in different ways. These alternative British pronunciations are given in the dictionary. Use your dictionary to find out the two possible British pronunciations of the following words:

1 controversy   _____   _____

2 finance   _____   _____

3 grass   _____   _____

4 montage   _____   _____

Word Stress

English word stress is very difficult to predict. In fact there are rules, but they are so complicated that it is probably best to learn the stress pattern of a word when you learn the word itself. In the dictionary, stress is shown by <u>underlining</u> the vowel in the stressed syllable.

1   Stress

Say the following words aloud and <u>underline</u> the vowel sound in the stressed syllable. Then check in the dictionary.

1	about	5	bad-tempered	9	enter	13	name-drop
2	area	6	banana	10	heavy metal	14	perhaps
3	arrive	7	camera	11	high street	15	potato
4	assembly line	8	chocolate	12	money-maker	16	receive

Word Stress (continued)

2 Stress and Parts of Speech

Some words in English have the same spelling, but their pronunciation changes depending on what part of speech they are. This pronunciation change is often one of stress. Look at this example from the dictionary:

contest (contests, contesting, contested)
☑ The noun is pronounced /kɒntest/. The verb is pronounced /kəntest/.

Read the following pairs of sentences aloud and then <u>underline</u> the stressed sound in the words in *italics*. Then check in the dictionary.

1 a   The *present* chairperson is a woman.

   b   Today I want to *present* the student view.

2 a   Keep a *record* of any repair bills.

   b   I'd just like to *record* my reservations about the decision.

3 a   He is perfectly *content* to remain living in Sweden.

   b   The *content* is irrelevant.

4 a   It has to have a building *permit*.

   b   His poor health wouldn't *permit* it.

5 a   The *object* of war is a more perfect peace.

   b   Would they *object* to you being an architect?

3 Unstressed Syllables

Unstressed syllables are not pronounced very clearly and are an important characteristic of English. Many unstressed syllables contain the vowel /ə/. The vowels /ɪ/ and /ʊ/ are also common in unstressed syllables and when these vowels can be pronounced in different ways, they are transcribed in *italic* script. They are called 'unprotected' vowels.

Say these words aloud and circle the vowel in the unstressed syllable. Then check in the dictionary.

1   photograph

2   doctor

3   report

4   paper

5   secret

6   release

7   better

Pronunciation, Spelling and Meaning

1   Different Pronunciation, Different Meaning, Same Spelling

Some words in English have the same spelling, but two different meanings and two different pronunciations. Read the following pairs of sentences aloud. Then write a phonetic transcription for each of the words in *italics*. Use the dictionary if you are unsure of the phonetic characters.

1   a   There was a fierce *wind* blowing.   _____

    b   *Wind* the wire round the screws.   _____

2   a   He opened the door with a *bow*.   _____

    b   Tie it in a *bow*.   _____

3   a   ...a gentleman in the second *row*.   _____

    b   We had a terrible *row* last night.   _____

2   Different Spellings, Different Meaning, Same Pronunciation

Look at the poem below. You will find lots of misspelled words. Read the words aloud. Can you recognize the words now? Rewrite the poem with the correct spellings — there are sixteen mistakes to find.

I have a spell chequer.   _____

It came with my PC.   _____

It plainly marks four my revue   _____

miss takes I cannot sea.   _____

I've run this poem threw it   _____

I'm shore your pleased too no.   _____

Its perfect in it's weigh   _____

my chequer tolled me sew.   _____

3   Same Pronunciation, Different Meaning, Different Spelling

These jokes are based on words which have the same pronunciation but a different spelling and meaning (homophones). Read these jokes and see if you can think of another word which has the same pronunciation as the word in *italics*. Write this word in the space provided.

1 What did the bell say when it fell in the water? I'm *wringing* wet.   _____

2 Estate Agent: This next house hasn't got a *flaw*.   _____

   Customer: What do you walk on then?

3 When is a shop like a boat? When it has *sales*.   _____

4 What vegetable needs a plumber? A *leek*.   _____

5 When is a yellow book not a yellow book? When it is *read*.   _____

SECTION 5: LOOKING AT MEANING

Synonyms and Antonyms

1   Synonyms

A synonym is a word which means the same, or nearly the same, as another word. Look at this sentence:

She was wearing a blue **pullover**.

In the Extra Column for the word **pullover** you will find = **jumper**. This tells you that the word **pullover** means the same as **jumper**, so they are synonyms here.

However, you cannot always substitute one word for the other in all contexts.

Look at the following words and see if you can think of synonyms for them. When you've finished, look them up in the dictionary.

Words	Synonyms		Words	Synonyms
1 air hostess	_____	4	illegal	_____
2 appalling	_____	5	jail	_____
3 catastrophe	_____	6	muddle	_____

2   Antonyms

An antonym is a word which means the opposite, or nearly the opposite, of another word. Look at this sentence:

How **careless** *of me.*

In the Extra Column for the word **careless** you will find ≠ **careful** next to paragraph 1. This tells you that the word **careless** means the opposite of **careful**, so they are antonyms here.

However, it does not mean that they are opposites in all contexts.

Look at the following words and see if you can think of antonyms for them. When you've finished, look them up in the dictionary.

Words	Antonyms		Words	Antonyms
1 beautiful	_____	4	heavily	_____
2 cheap	_____	5	introvert	_____
3 hatred	_____	6	profit	_____

Opposites and Compounds

1 Forming Opposites of Words

There are a number of different prefixes which are used to form words which mean the opposite, or more or less the opposite, of other words. For example, the opposite of **possible** is **impossible**; the opposite of **approve** is **disapprove**. You can, of course, also make an opposite meaning by using **not**; for example, **not possible** and **not approve** or even **not impossible** and **not disapprove**.

Here are some common prefixes:

un-   in-   im-   il-   ir-   dis-   mis-

Using these prefixes, give the opposite of the words in the list below. Then look up the words you have made in the dictionary to check whether you are right.

	Words	Opposites			Words	Opposites
1	happy	_____	6		religious	_____
2	discreet	_____	7		manage	_____
3	legal	_____	8		patient	_____
4	reversible	_____	9		direct	_____
5	moral	_____	10		pleasure	_____

2 Compounds

Which of these words can be joined together to form new words? For example, **black** and **board** can be joined together to form **blackboard**. When you've finished, check in the dictionary to see whether you are right.

1	~~black~~	quake	**blackboard** _____
2	pan	bow	_____
3	green	~~board~~	_____
4	earth	suit	_____
5	rain	house	_____
6	push	cake	_____
7	swim	chair	_____ _____

Words with Multiple Meanings

Many of the most common words in English have many different meanings. This can be confusing when you know one meaning of a word and not the others.

1   Multiple Meanings

Complete the examples below with the words from the box, choosing one word which fits in the gaps in all three examples. When you've finished, check your answers by looking up the headword in the dictionary. The first one has been done for you.

| post   deal   blow   mean   mind |

1   The bushes and trees were **blowing** in the wind.

A guard was **blowing** his whistle.

Tourism was dealt a severe **blow** by Hurricane Andrew.

2   I'd feel _____ saying no.

Managing well _____ communicating well.

The red signal _____ you can shoot.

3   I hope you don't _____ me calling in like this, without an appointment.

Jim Coulters will _____ the store while I'm away.

There was no doubt in his _____ that the man was serious.

4   You have to get eight wooden _____ and drive them into the ground.

Sir Peter has held several senior military _____.

The winner will be notified by _____.

5   I am in a position to save you a good _____ of time.

Japan will have to do a _____ with America on rice imports.

They _____ in antiques.

2   Puns and Meanings

Many jokes, especially children's jokes, depend on puns. A pun is a clever or amusing use of a word or phrase with two meanings, or of words with the same sound but different meanings. Read these jokes and look up the *italic* words in the dictionary to check their different meanings. Then write down the paragraph numbers for the 2 different meanings of the words.

Jokes   **Paragraphs**

1   Why did the banana go out with the prune?
    Because he couldn't find a *date*.   _____

2   What happens to fruit and vegetables in autumn?
    People eat what they *can*, and *can* what they can't.   _____

3   Have your eyes ever been *checked*?
    No, they've always been this colour.   _____

4   Teacher: I hear you *missed* school yesterday.
    Sam: Not one bit.   _____

Pragmatics

Pragmatics refer to a person's intention when using language. There are several types of pragmatic information given in the dictionary and pages xxii-xxiii of the Introduction to the dictionary give an example and explanation of each of them.

In the Extra Column in the dictionary you will often see a box describing different types of pragmatics, e.g. feelings, approval, disapproval, emphasis. This is to draw your attention to the fact that this word or phrase conveys something which is over and above the basic meaning of the word or phrase.

Look at the entry for **actually**:

> **actually** /ˈæktʃuəli/ ◆◆◆◆◆
>
> **1** You use **actually** to indicate that a situation exists or happened, or to emphasize that it is true. ❑ *One afternoon, I grew bored and actually fell asleep for a few minutes... Interest is only payable on the amount actually borrowed.*
> ADV:
> ADV before v, ADV group
> emphasis
>
> **2** You use **actually** when you are correcting or contradicting someone. ❑ *No, I'm not a student. I'm a doctor, actually... 'So it's not a family show then?'—'Well, actually, I think that's exactly what it is.'*
> ADV:
> ADV with cl
> emphasis
>
> **3** You can use **actually** when you are politely expressing an opinion that other people might not have expected from you. ❑ *'Do you think it's a good idea to socialize with one's patients?'—'Actually, I do, I think it's a great idea.'... I would be surprised, actually, if he left Birmingham.*
> ADV:
> ADV with cl
> politeness
>
> **4** You use **actually** to introduce a new topic into a conversation. ❑ *Well actually, John, I rang you for some advice... Actually, let's just read this little bit where you've made them bump into each other.*
> ADV:
> ADV with cl

Three of the four paragraphs show pragmatic information in the Extra Column. This is because the word **actually** is doing certain things in the language which are difficult to describe in terms of meaning alone. The definitions are describing when you use the word **actually**, rather than just explaining its meaning. You should pay particular attention to this type of definition.

Here are some examples of **actually** taken from The Bank of English. Match them with the correct paragraph number above.

	Examples	**Paragraph**
1	No, a Dutch firm, actually. A big one.	_____
2	Actually, Dan, before I forget, she asked me to give you this.	_____
3	Do you actually encourage children to talk about divorce?	_____
4	I can't believe Dr Morgan is actually going to retire.	_____
5	I'd quite like a flat actually. It's cheaper as well.	_____
6	I think it's a disastrous influence actually but that's only my opinion.	_____
7	Actually, I didn't come here just to help you with the party.	_____
8	Actually, in the negotiations, our experience was quite different.	_____

Turn to the entry for **life** in the dictionary and look at the pragmatic information that is given there for the different meanings.

SECTION 6: LOOKING AT VERY COMMON WORDS

Get, Have and Take

Some of the most common words in the English language are used in many different ways. As a result, the dictionary entries for these words are often long and detailed. The exercises in this section are designed to give you practice in the skills you need to use these entries efficiently.

1   Get

Get is a very complicated verb. There are over 40 subentries for **get** in the dictionary and over two pages of phrasal verbs formed with **get**! To make it easier for you to find the information you need, the entries have been divided into sections, with a 'menu' at the top of the entry to help you decide which section you need to look at.

```
                    get
① CHANGING, CAUSING, MOVING, OR
   REACHING
② OBTAINING, RECEIVING, OR CATCH-
   ING
③ PHRASES AND PHRASAL VERBS
```

Look at these examples and decide which section you would find them in. Then check in the dictionary.

Examples	**Section**
1 He had been having trouble getting a hotel room.	_____
2 ... the ravishing island of Ischia, where rich Italians get away from it all.	_____
3 You don't seem to get the point.	_____
4 There's no point in getting upset.	_____
5 It was dark by the time she got home.	_____

2   Have

a   Different Meanings

Have is also a very complicated verb. There are 28 subentries for **have** in the dictionary. To make life easier for you, **have** also has a 'menu' at the top of the entry to help you decide which section you need to look at.

```
                   have
① AUXILIARY VERB USES
② USED WITH NOUNS DESCRIBING AC-
   TIONS
③ OTHER VERB USES AND PHRASES
④ MODAL PHRASES
```

Look at these examples and decide which section you would find them in. Then check in the dictionary.

Examples	**Section**
1 They didn't have to pay tax.	_____
2 What have you found so far?	_____
3 Do you have any brothers or sisters?	_____
4 I'll have a think about that.	_____

Get, Have and Take (continued)

b   With Nouns

Have is used in combinations with a wide range of nouns, where the meaning of the combination is mostly given by the noun. People are more likely to use these combinations than a more specific verb. In the following sentences the 'have combinations' have been replaced by more specific verbs and although the sentences are grammatically correct, some of them sound a bit strange. Rewrite the sentences using a 'have combination'. For example, *She breakfasted at 7 o'clock* is much less common than *She had breakfast at 7 o'clock*.

1   Did you look at the shop when you were here?   _____

2   I'm going to shower.   _____

3   That Tuesday, Lorna lunched in her room.   _____

4   Sit down and rest.   _____

5   She walked in the park.   _____

6   We quarrelled yesterday.   _____

3   Take

a   With Nouns

Take is a complicated verb that is used in many different ways. As with **get** and **have**, **take** has been divided into sections, with a 'menu' at the top of the entry to help you decide which section you need to look at.

take
① USED WITH NOUNS DESCRIBING ACTIONS
② OTHER USES

Read the following sentences. They do not always sound like natural English. Rewrite each one by adding the verb **take**, changing a verb into a noun, and making any other changes that are needed in the structure. For example, *He looked briefly at his notes* is more frequently expressed as *He took a brief look at his notes*.

1   He stepped towards Jack.   _____

2   She is always quick to be offended.   _____

3   I photographed him magnificently.   _____

4   Let's break here for a few minutes.   _____

5   Nuns still vow poverty and celibacy   _____

     and obedience.   _____

Get, Have and Take (continued)

b   Other Uses

Read the following sentences. Each example has had one word changed — the verb
take has been replaced by another verb with a similar meaning. Find the verb and
replace it with an appropriate form of **take**.

1   He removed a cigarette from the box on the
     table.   _____

2   By all means have a day or two to think
     about it.   _____

3   Let me have your coat.   _____

In each of these examples, one or more words can be replaced by **take**. Rewrite the
examples using **take**.

4   If we consider wealth as a whole, then
     women are a long way below average.   _____

5   Some people change the world —
     think of Ghandi, for example.   _____

6   What about Spain? It's the most immediate
     case.   _____

Who, Which and That

1   Who or Which

Compare **who** and **which** in the dictionary. What are the most important differences
between them? Now complete the following examples with either **who** or **which**.

1   _____ school do you go to?

2   _____'s that? Is it your sister?

3   We have two televisions, one of _____ is black and white.

4   And then it rained, _____ was a pity.

5   My brother, _____ is eighteen, is training to be a hairdresser.

6   _____ of those books do you like best?

7   _____ of your teachers do you like most?

2   Who and That

In which of the following sentences can **that** be substituted for **who**?

1   Is that the boy who used to stay with you?

2   Who looks after the children?

3   It wasn't me who suggested we should meet here!

4   I recently spoke to Dr Smith, who is a specialist in European affairs.

5   ...the girl who wants to marry you.

6   I don't know who his dentist is.

SECTION 1: FINDING WORDS AND PHRASES

Alphabetical Ordering

1	destruction
2	destructive
3	disintegrate
4	disinterested
5	distinctive
6	distinguished
7	distortion
8	distribution
9	distributor
10	district

Compounds

1	1	bread
	2	bread and butter
	3	breadboard
	4	breadth
	5	breakdown
	6	breakfast
	7	breakfast television
	8	breakfast time
	9	break-in
	10	breaking point

2	1	nightclub, night club
	2	nightgown
	3	nightlife, night-life
	4	nightmare
	5	night owl
	6	night-time, night time
	7	nightwatchman, night-watchman
	8	applesauce
	9	checkup
	10	knickknacks
	11	markup

Spelling

1	1	*a*ffected	
	2	*e*ffect	
	3	*e*ffect	
	4	*a*ffects	
	5	*a*ffect	

2	1	a	principal
		b	principle
	2	a	practise
		b	practice
	3	a	stationary
		b	stationery
	4	a	complement
		b	compliment

Phrases 1

1	blessing
2	old
3	gut
4	game
5	matter

Phrases 2

1	blind, 11, turn a blind eye
2	eye, 25, keep an eye on
3	eye, 13, catch your eye
4	eye, 14, catch someone's eye
5	wool, 4, pull the wool over your eyes
6	eye, 18, cry your eyes out
7	black eye, black eye
8	naked, 7, the naked eye

Phrases 3

1	In view of
2	with a view to
3	in my view
4	on view
5	in view
6	In my view

Phrasal Verbs

1	1	2
	2	1
	3	5, 6
	4	1
	5	break through
	6	breakable
	7	break away, break down, break in, break into, break off, break out, break through, break up

2	1	2
	2	4
	3	1
	4	3

SECTION 2: USING THE EXPLANATIONS AND EXAMPLES

Someone and Something

1	a
2	a and b
3	b
4	a

Word Order

1	1	We are incomparably better off than we were a year ago.
	2	They don't go out much, particularly during the winter months.
	3	The film was incredibly boring.

2	1	small French
	2	soft yellow
	3	Huge gilt
	4	white woollen
	5	long unbroken
	6	old pink check

Verbs

1	1	A
	2	A
	3	B
	4	A
	5	C
	6	C

2	1	A
	2	A
	3	B
	4	A
	5	B

Collocations 1

1	1	weather, temperatures, day
	2	task, prospect, commitment, responsibility
	3	hair
	4	building, factory
	5	work

2	1	asleep
	2	success
	3	rich
	4	broke

Collocations 2

1	making a telephone call
2	do homework
3	made a mistake
4	set an example
5	do some shopping
6	make, do
7	making, making
8	makes *or* gives
9	gives
10	hold

Style and Usage 1

1	1	BRIT
	2	mainly AM
	3	OLD-FASHIONED
	4	FORMAL
	5	LEGAL
	6	MEDICAL
	7	INFORMAL
	8	TECHNICAL
	9	WRITTEN
	10	LITERARY

2	1	b
	2	a
	3	b
	4	b

Style and Usage 2

1	British, faucet
2	American, bonnet
3	British, trunk
4	American, pavement
5	British, pants
6	American, petrol
7	American, lift
8	British, line
9	British, cookie
10	American, dustbin

SECTION 3: USING THE GRAMMATICAL INFORMATION

Parts of Speech

1 1 dictionary, information, meaning, words, grammar
2 give, gives, is shown
3 useful
4 just, also, clearly, concisely
5 about, of, in

2 1 a down: preposition
 b down: verb
 c down: adverb
 2 a good: adjective
 b good: noun
 3 a round: noun
 b round: adjective
 c round: preposition
 d round: verb

Verbs

1 1 V n n
2 V to-inf
3 V n
4 V prep/adv
5 V with quote
6 V pron-refl
7 V that
8 V n adj
9 V n to-inf
10 V n *into* -ing
11 V
12 V -ing

2 1 about
2 to
3 on
4 on
5 on
6 about
7 for
8 from
9 to
10 on
11 in

Nouns 1

1 1 N-UNCOUNT
2 N-VAR
3 N-VAR
4 N-COUNT

2 1 lack
2 paperback

Nouns 2

1 1 N to-inf
2 poss N
3 N n
4 N *for* n
5 n N

2 1 a which most parents will find appealing
 b same
 2 a humanitarian
 b theatre
 3 a his
 b of the mass-produced automobile

Adjectives 1

1 1 a ADJ-GRADED
 b ADJ
 2 a ADJ
 b ADJ-GRADED
 3 a ADJ-GRADED
 b ADJ

2 1 both
2 ADJ n
3 ADJ n
4 v-link ADJ
5 both
6 v-link ADJ

Adjectives 2

1 1 ADJ *to* n
2 ADJ that
3 ADJ to-inf
4 *it* v-link ADJ to-inf
5 ADJ *of* n

2 1 c 3 a 5 f 7 d
 2 g 4 b 6 e

Adverbs

1 1 ADV with cl
2 ADV with v
3 ADV adj/adv
4 ADV -ed

2 1 ADV adv/prep
2 ADV *about/going* to-inf
3 ADV n
4 ADV before v

ANSWERS

SECTION 4: USING THE PHONETICS

Consonants and Vowels

1	1	/ʒ/
	2	/dʒ/
	3	/j/
	4	/tʃ/
	5	/ʃ/
	6	/θ/
	7	/ð/
	8	/ŋ/

2	a	1	/ɪ/, 5
		2	/ʊ/, 3
		3	/e/, 5
		4	/æ/, 4
		5	/ʌ/, 4
		6	/ə/, 3
		7	/ɒ/, 4
		8	/u/, 3
		9	/i/, 3

	b	1	/iː/, 3
		2	/ɔː/, 4
		3	/ɑː/, 4
		4	/ɜː/, 5
		5	/uː/, 5

	c	1	/ʊə/, 3
		2	/aɪə/, 2
		3	/aʊ/, 4
		4	/aʊə/, 2
		5	/ɪə/, 3
		6	/eə/, 4
		7	/eɪ/, 5
		8	/oʊ/, 3
		9	/ɔɪ/, 3
		10	/aɪ/, 6

American and British Pronunciation

1	1	AM, BRIT
	2	BRIT, AM
	3	AM, BRIT
	4	BRIT, AM
	5	AM, BRIT

2	1	/kɒntɹəvɜ.ʳsi/	/kɒntrɒvəˈsi/
	2	/faɪnæns/	/fɪnæns/
	3	/grɑːs/	/græs/
	4	/mɒntɑːʒ/	/mɒntɑːʒ/

Word Stress

1	1		about
	2		area
	3		arrive
	4		assembly line
	5		bad-tempered
	6		banana
	7		camera
	8		chocolate
	9		enter
	10		heavy metal
	11		high street
	12		money-maker
	13		name-drop
	14		perhaps
	15		potato
	16		receive

2	1	a	present
		b	present
	2	a	record
		b	record
	3	a	content
		b	content
	4	a	permit
		b	permit
	5	a	object
		b	object

3	1	photograph
	2	doctor
	3	report
	4	paper
	5	secret
	6	release
	7	better

38

SECTION 4: USING THE PHONETICS (continued)

Pronunciation, Spelling and Meaning

1   1   a   /wɪnd/
          b   /waɪnd/
     2   a   /baʊ/
          b   /boʊ/
     3   a   /roʊ/
          b   /raʊ/

3   1   ringing
     2   floor
     3   sails
     4   leak
     5   red

2   I have a spell <u>checker</u>.
     It came with my PC.
     It plainly marks <u>for</u> my <u>review</u>
     <u>mistakes</u> I cannot <u>see</u>.
     I've run this poem <u>through</u> it
     I'm <u>sure</u> <u>you're</u> pleased <u>to</u> <u>know</u>.
     <u>It's</u> perfect in <u>its</u> <u>way</u>
     My <u>checker</u> <u>told</u> me <u>so</u>.

SECTION 5: LOOKING AT MEANING

Synonyms and Antonyms

1   1   stewardess
     2   dreadful
     3   disaster
     4   unlawful
     5   prison
     6   mess, confusion

2   1   ugly
     2   expensive, dear
     3   love
     4   lightly
     5   extrovert
     6   loss

Opposites and Compounds

1   1   unhappy
     2   indiscreet
     3   illegal
     4   irreversible
     5   immoral
     6   irreligious
     7   mismanage
     8   impatient
     9   indirect
     10   displeasure

2   1   blackboard
     2   pancake
     3   greenhouse
     4   earthquake
     5   rainbow
     6   pushchair
     7   swimsuit

SECTION 5: LOOKING AT MEANING (continued)

Words with Multiple Meanings

1	1	blowing, blowing, blow
	2	mean, means, means
	3	mind, mind, mind
	4	posts, posts, post
	5	deal, deal, deal
2	1	8 & 11
	2	can 1, para. 2 & can 2, para. 2
	3	check, para. 1 & checked
	4	miss 2, para. 9 & 7

Pragmatics

1	2
2	4
3	1
4	1
5	1
6	3
7	4
8	2

SECTION 6: LOOKING AT VERY COMMON WORDS

Get, Have and Take

1	1	2	
	2	3	
	3	2	
	4	1	
	5	1	
2	a	1	4
		2	1
		3	3
		4	2
	b	1	have a look
		2	have a shower
		3	had lunch
		4	have a rest
		5	had a walk
		6	had a quarrel

3 a 1 He took a step towards Jack
2 She is always quick to take offence.
3 I took a magnificent photoqraph/photo of him.
4 Let's take a break here for a few minutes.
5 Nuns still take vows of poverty and celibacy and obedience.

3 b 1 He took a cigarette from the box on the table.
2 By all means take a day or two to think about it.
3 Let me take your coat.
4 If we take wealth as a whole, then women are a long way below average.
5 Some people change the world — take Ghandi, for example.
6 Take Spain. It's the most immediate case.

Who, Which and That

1	1	which
	2	who
	3	which
	4	which
	5	who
	6	which
	7	which
2	1, 3, 5	